Weight

Julie Murray

Abdo Kids Junior
is an Imprint of Abdo Kids
abdobooks.com

Abdo
MEASURE IT!
Kids

abdobooks.com

Published by Abdo Kids, a division of ABDO, P.O. Box 398166, Minneapolis, Minnesota 55439.
Copyright © 2020 by Abdo Consulting Group, Inc. International copyrights reserved in all countries.
No part of this book may be reproduced in any form without written permission from the publisher.
Abdo Kids Junior™ is a trademark and logo of Abdo Kids.

Printed in the United States of America, North Mankato, Minnesota.

052019

092019

THIS BOOK CONTAINS
RECYCLED MATERIALS

Photo Credits: iStock, Shutterstock

Production Contributors: Teddy Borth, Jennie Forsberg, Grace Hansen

Design Contributors: Christina Doffing, Candice Keimig, Dorothy Toth

Library of Congress Control Number: 2018963317

Publisher's Cataloging-in-Publication Data

Names: Murray, Julie, author.

Title: Weight / by Julie Murray.

Description: Minneapolis, Minnesota : Abdo Kids, 2020 | Series: Measure it! |
    Includes online resources and index.

Identifiers: ISBN 9781532185335 (lib. bdg.) | ISBN 9781532186318 (ebook) |
    ISBN 9781532186806 (Read-to-me ebook)

Subjects: LCSH: Weights and measures--Juvenile literature. | Size and shape--
    Juvenile literature. | Measurement--Juvenile literature.

Classification: DDC 530.813--dc23

Table of Contents

Weight

Weight is how **heavy** or **light** something is.

A scale is a tool.

It measures weight.

The ball is light.

It is 1 pound (lb).

Wes is on the scale.

He is 56 lbs (25.4 kg).

The dog is heavy.

It is 110 lbs (50 kg).

Ounces (oz) are light. A slice of bread is 1 oz (28 g).

Very heavy things are in tons.

The bus is 15 tons (13,608 kg).

The elephant is

5 tons (4,536 kg).

This scale **compares** weight.

Which side weighs more?

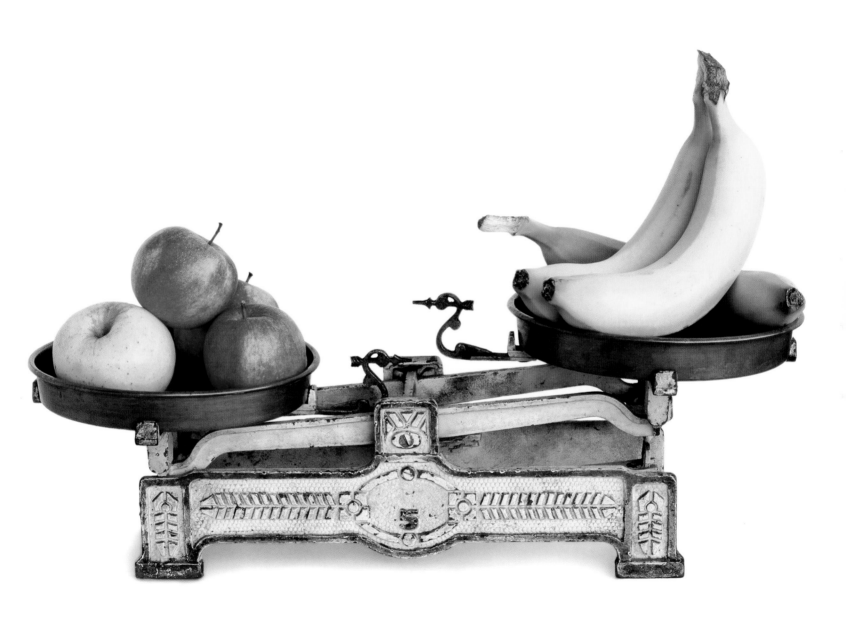

Let's Review!

light

heavy

measure using
ounces
(oz)

measure using
pounds
(lb)

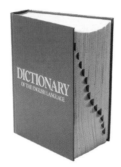  

measure using
tons
(T)

Glossary

heavy
of great weight.

compare
to bring together to learn the similarities and differences.

light
not heavy.

Index

Abdo Kids ONLINE
FREE! ONLINE MULTIMEDIA RESOURCES

Visit **abdokids.com** to access crafts, games, videos, and more!

Use Abdo Kids code **MWK5335** or scan this QR code!